1300+ Jokes
Animal Jokes for Kids

Johnny B. Laughing

CONTENTS

Aardvark Jokes

Q: Did you hear about the household appliance that eats ants and records TV shows?

A: It's the VCRdvark!

Q: Which aardvark holds the speed record?

A: The nearsighted aardvark, who wrapped his tongue around a motorcycle!

Q: What has six legs, two arms, four eyes, and a tail?

A: A man holding an aardvark.

Q: What has a long nose, wears a mask, and sits tall in the saddle?

A: The Lone Aardvark!

Q: What do you call a Polish aardvark?

A: A Polaark!

Q: What did the impatient waiter ask the gluttonous aardvark?

A: Is that your final ant, sir!

Q: How many aardvarks can ride on an elephant?

A: Six... three on the back and three in the trunk!

Q: What do you call an aardvark that's good at golf?

A: A paredvark!

Q: What do you call a road construction aardvark?

A: A tarredvark!

Q: What do you call an aardvark astronaut?

A: A starredvark!

Q: What do you call a three-footed aardvark?

A: A yardvark!

Q: When is an aardvark jumpy?

A: When he's got ants in his pants!

Q: Why do aardvarks make undesirable neighbors?

A: Because they always have their noses in other people's business!

Q: Why does mama aardvark call her husband a cannibal?

A: Because he ate his ant for dinner!

Q: Who won the animal race?

A: The giraffe and the aardvark were running neck and neck, but the aardvark won by a nose!

Q: What did the aardvark say when he lost the race to the ant?

A: If you can't beat 'em, eat 'em!

Q: Why can elephants swim - and aardvarks can't?

A: Aardvarks don't have trunks!

Q: What do you call an aardvark that is good with a light saber?

A: A darthvark!

Q: What do you call a thick-skinned aardvark?

A: A hardvark!

Q: What do you call an aardvark that plays poker?

A: A cardvark!

Q: What do you call an aardvark in a frying pan?

A: A lardvark!

Q: What do you call a pickled aardvark?

A: A jarredvark!

Q: What do you call an aardvark that works security?

A: A guardvark!

Q: What do you call an aardvark that's been thrown out of a pub?

A: A barredvark!

Q: What do you call an aardvark that's just lost a fight?

A: A vark!

Q: What do you call an aardvark that's just won a fight?

A: A well 'aardvark!

Q: What do you call a boxing match between two aardvarks?

A: A snout bout!

Q: Where does the aardvark family always come first?

A: In the phone book!

Q: Why was Easter the aardvark's favorite holiday?

A: Because he liked aard-boiled eggs!

Q: What has 200 legs, 50 noses, and is very loud?

A: A herd of stampeding aardvarks!

Q: Why do aardvarks like to talk to ants?

A: They can stick to the subject!

Q: How do ants hide from aardvarks?

A: They disguise themselves as uncles!

Q: What command does the aardvark give most often when he sails?

A: Snout about!

Q: What does an aardvark use when he has a cold?

A: An ant-ihistamine!

Q: What's worse than a giraffe with a sore throat?

A: An aardvark with the sniffles!

Q: Who's aardvark's favorite male singer?
A: Frank Sinostril!

Q: What does an aardvark take for ant-digestion?
A: Anta-Seltzer!

Q: Who's the aardvark's favorite female vocalist?
A: Bearbara Streis-ant!

Q: What does an aardvark get when he overeats?
A: Ant-digestion!

Bird Jokes

Q: Why did the chicken say meow, oink, bow-wow, and moo?
A: He was studying foreign languages.

Q: What is the difference between a fly and a bird?
A: A bird can fly, but a fly can't bird!

Q: What birds are found in Portugal?
A: Portu-geese!

Q: What is the strongest bird?
A: A crane!

Q: Why does a flamingo lift up one leg?
A: Because if he lifted up both legs he would fall over!

Q: What do you call a chicken that crosses the road without looking both ways?
A: Dead.

Q: What happens when you drop a hand gren-egg?
A: It eggs-plodes!

Q: What do you call the outside of a hand gren-egg?
A: The bombshell!

Q: What do you get when a chicken lays an egg on top of a barn?
A: An eggroll!

Q: What do chickens serve at birthday parties?
A: Coop-cakes!

Q: Is chicken soup good for your health?
A: Not if you're the chicken!

Q: Why did the chick disappoint his mother?
A: He wasn't what he was cracked up to be!

Q: What did one chicken say to the other after they walked through poison ivy?
A: You scratch my beak and I'll scratch yours!

Q: What do chicken families do on Saturday afternoon?
A: They go on peck-nics!

Q: Why did the chicken cross the road half way?

A: He wanted to lay it on the line!

Q: What did the chicken do when she saw a bucket of fried chicken?

A: She kicked the bucket!

Q: What happened when the chicken ate cement?

A: She laid a sidewalk!

Q: What happens when a hen eats gunpowder?

A: She lays hand gren-eggs!

Q: Why is it easy for chicks to talk?

A: Because talk is cheep!

Q: Why don't chickens like people?

A: They beat eggs!

Q: What do you get when you cross a chicken with a duck?

A: A bird that lies down!

Q: What happened to the chicken whose feathers were all pointing the wrong way?

A: She was tickled to death!

Q: What do you call a crazy chicken?
A: A cuckoo cluck!

Q: Why did the chicken end up in the soup?
A: Because it ran out of cluck!

Q: How long do chickens work?
A: Around the cluck!

Q: Why does a chicken coop have two doors?
A: Because if had four doors it would be a chicken sedan!

Q: What do you call a rooster who wakes you up at the same time every morning?
A: An alarm cluck!

Q: Why did the chicken cross the net?
A: It wanted to get to the other site!

Q: Why did the chicken cross the playground?
A: To get to the other slide!

Q: Why didn't the chicken skeleton cross the road?
A: Because he didn't have enough guts!

Q: Why did the turkey cross the road?
A: To prove he wasn't chicken!

Q: Why did the chicken cross the basketball court?
A: He heard the referee calling fowls!

Q: What is the definition of Robin?
A: A bird who steals!

Q: Why did the parrot wear a raincoat?
A: Because she wanted to be a Polly unsaturated!

Q: What kind of birds do you usually find locked up?
A: Jail-birds!

Q: What did they call the canary that flew into the pastry dish?
A: Tweetie Pie!

Q: What do you get if your budgie flies into the blender?
A: Shredded Tweet!

Q: What do you get if you cross a parrot with a centipede?
A: A great walkie-talkie!

Q: What do you get if you cross a woodpecker with a carrier pigeon?
A: A bird who knocks before delivering its message!

Q: What happened when the owl lost his voice?
A: He didn't give a hoot!

Q: What happens when ducks fly upside down?
A: They quack up!

Q: What do you get if you cross a parrot with a woodpecker?
A: A bird that talks in Morse code!

Q: Where do birds invest their money?
A: In the stork market!

Q: What do you call a bird that lives underground?
A: A mynah bird!

Q: What do you get if you cross a parrot with a shark?
A: Birds that will talk you ear off!

Q: What is a duck's favorite TV show?
A: The feather forecast!

Q: What kind of bird opens doors?
A: A kiwi!

Q: What flies through the jungle singing opera?
A: The parrots of Penzance!

Q: What do owls sing when it is raining?
A: Too wet to woo!

Q: What's another name for a clever duck?
A: A wise quacker!

Q: What bird tastes just like butter?
A: A stork!

Q: What do you give a sick bird?
A: Tweetment!

Q: What do parrots eat?
A: Polyfilla!

Q: What is a parrot's favorite game?
A: Hide and speak!

Q: What do you call a Scottish parrot?
A: A Macaw!

Q: What do you get if you cross a duck with a firework?
A: A firequaker!

Q: What language do birds speak?
A: Pigeon English!

Q: How do you get a parrot to talk properly?
A: Send him to polytechnic!

Q: What do you call a crate of ducks?
A: A box of quackers!

Q: Why didn't the owl, owl?
A: Because the woodpecker would peck her!

Q: What's got six legs and can fly long distances?
A: Three swallows!

Q: Which bird is always out of breath?
A: A puffin!

Q: What do you call a bunch of chickens playing hide-and-seek?

A: Fowl play!

Q: What is green and pecks on trees?

A: Woody Wood Pickle!

Q: How does a bird with a broken wing manage to land safely?

A: With its sparrowchute!

Q: Where do birds meet for coffee?

A: In a nest-cafe!

Q: What do you call a very rude bird?

A: A mockingbird!

Q: Why is a sofa like a roast chicken?

A: Because they're both full of stuffing!

Q: How do you get a cut-price parrot?

A: Plant birdseed!

Q: When is the best time to buy budgies?

A: When they're going cheap!

Q: What do you call a woodpecker with no beak?

A: A head banger!

Q: What birds spend all their time on their knees?
A: Birds of prey!

Q: What is a polygon?
A: A dead parrot!

Q: What's brown and white and flies everywhere?
A: Thanksgiving turkey, when you carve it with a chain saw!

Q: What do you get if you cross a nun and a chicken?
A: A pecking order.

Q: How do you identify a bald eagle?
A: All his feathers are combed over to one side.

Q: Why did the rooster cross the road?
A: To get to the chick across the street!

Q: What geometric figure is like a runaway parrot?
A: A polygon.

Q: What's the definition of parity?
A: Two parrots exactly the same!

Q: What profession did the parrot get into when it swallowed the clock?

A: Politics.

Q: Where do blind parrots go for treatment?

A: The birds eye counter!

Q: What do you get if you cross a bee with a parrot?

A: An animal that's always telling you how busy it is!

Q: Where do the cleverest parrots live?

A: In the brain tree forests!

Q: What did the baby owls parents say when he wanted to go to a party?

A: You're not owld enough.

Q: What do confused owls say?

A: Too-whit-to-why?

Q: What does an educated owl say?

A: Whom.

Q: What do you get if you cross an eagle with a skunk?

A: A bird that stinks to high heaven.

Q: How do you make a tame duck wild?
A: Annoy it.

Q: Why were the hens lying on their backs with their legs in the air?
A: Because eggs were going up!

Q: What happens when geese land in a volcano?
A: They cook their own gooses!

Q: Why does a rooster watch TV?
A: For hentertainment!

Q: What do you get if you cross a chicken with a cement mixer?
A: A brick-layer!

Q: Why do ducks have webbed feet?
A: To stamp out forest fires!

Q: What do you get from a drunken chicken?
A: Scotch eggs!

Q: What kind of bird lays electric eggs?
A: A battery hen!

Q: How do you stop a rooster crowing on Sunday?

A: Eat him on Saturday!

Q: What did the baby chick say when he saw his mother sitting on an orange?

A: Dad, dad, look what marma-laid!

Q: What goes peck, bang, peck, bang, peck, bang?

A: A bunch of chickens in a field full of balloons!

Q: What is the definition of a goose?

A: An animal that grows down as it grows up!

Q: Why did the rooster run away?

A: He was chicken!

Q: What is a parrot?

A: A wordy birdy!

Q: Whose parrot sits on his shoulder shouting, pieces of four?

A: Short John Silver!

Q: What's orange and sounds like a parrot?

A: A carrot!

Q: Why did the bird join the air force?
A: He wanted to be a parrot trooper!

Q: Why is politics for the birds?
A: Because politicians always parrot the same old lines!

Q: What's a parrot's favorite song?
A: I love Parrots in the springtime!

Q: What are parrots favorite literary characters?
A: Mr. Macawber and Pollyanna!

Q: What's a parrot's favorite game?
A: Monopoly!

Q: How can you tell if a parrot is intelligent?
A: It speaks in Polly-syllables!

Q: Which bird ran for President?
A: H. Ross Parrot

Q: Why do parrots carry umbrellas?
A: So they don't become Polly-saturated!

Q: What did the parrot say when he saw a duck?

A: Polly want a quacker!

Q: What did the rich socialites parrot say?

A: Polly wants a cracker, with caviar please!

Q: What did the parrot say on Independence Day?

A: Polly wants a firecracker!

Q: What do you call the place where parrots make films?

A: Pollywood!

Q: What's the definition of Polystyrene?

A: A plastic parrot!

Q: Why did the man's pet vulture not make a sound for five years?

A: It was stuffed.

Q: What do you get if you cross a giant, hairy monster with a penguin?

A: I don't know, but it's a very tightfitting tuxedo.

Q: What kind of doctor does a duck visit?

A: A ducktor.

Q: Did you hear about the chicken that wanted to take ballet lessons?

A: He wanted to be a hentertainer.

Q: Why do seagulls fly over the sea?

A: Because if they flew over the bay, they'd be baygulls (bagels, get it?).

Q: Why did the chicken cross the road in Missouri?

A: To show the opossum it could be done.

Bug Jokes

Q: What's a bee-line?

A: The shortest distance between two buzz-stops!

Q: What is the biggest ant in the world?

A: An elephant!

Q: What lives in gum trees?

A: Stick insects!

Q: What has four wheels and flies?

A: A rubbish bin!

Q: What kind of suit does a bee wear to work?

A: A buzzness suit!

Q: What do you call a bee that's had a spell put on him?

A: He's bee-witched!

Q: What do bees do if they want to use public transport?

A: Wait at a buzz stop!

Q: Where would you put an injured insect?
A: In an antbulance!

Q: What is a bee's favorite classical music composer?
A: Bee-thoven!

Q: What does a queen bee do when she burps?
A: Issues a royal pardon!

Q: What goes hum-choo, hum choo?
A: A bee with a cold!

Q: How do fireflies lose weight?
A: They burn calories.

Q: How can you make a moth ball?
A: Hit it with a fly swatter.

Q: What do you get when you cross a bell with a bee?
A: A humdinger.

Q: What happened to the man who turned into an insect?
A: He just beetled off!

Q: What's black, yellow and covered in blackberries?

A: A bramble bee!

Q: What's more dangerous than being with a fool?

A: Fooling with a bee!

Q: Why did the bee started talking poetry?

A: He was waxing lyrical!

Q: Who writes books for little bees?

A: Bee-trix Potter!

Q: What did the bee say to the naughty bee?

A: Bee-hive yourself!

Q: What is the difference between an elephant and a flea?

A: An elephant can have fleas but a flea cant have elephants!

Q: How does a queen bee get around her hive?

A: She's throne!

Q: What is the difference between a flea bitten dog and a bored visitor?
A: Ones going to itch and the other are itching to go!

Q: How do fleas travel?
A: Itch hiking!

Q: What kinds of bugs bother sporting dogs?
A: Ath-fleats!

Q: What do you get from a bee that has an udder?
A: Milk and honey.

Q: What did the wife spider say to her husband when he tried to explain why he was late?
A: Your spinning me a yarn here!

Q: Why are spiders like tops?
A: They are always spinning!

Q: What kind of doctors are like spiders?
A: Spin doctors!

Q: What would happen if tarantulas were as big as horses?

A: If one bit you, you could ride it to hospital!

Q: What do you call 100 spiders on a tire?

A: A spinning wheel!

Q: What is a spider's favorite TV show?

A: The newly web game!

Q: What do you call a big Irish spider?

A: Paddy long legs!

Q: What are spiders webs good for?

A: Spiders!

Q: How do you spot a modern spider?

A: He doesn't have a web. He had a website!

Q: What did the spider say to the fly?

A: We're getting married. Do you want to come to the webbing?

Q: What is red and dangerous?

A: Strawberry and tarantula jelly!

Q: Why are spider's good swimmers?
A: They have webbed feet!

Q: What does a spider do when he gets angry?
A: He goes up the wall!

Q: Why did the spider buy a car?
A: So he could take it out for a spin!

Q: What do you get if you cross a tarantula with a rose?
A: I'm not sure, but I wouldn't try smelling it!

Q: What happened when the chef found a daddy long legs in the salad?
A: It became a daddy short legs!

Q: What did the spider say when he broke his new web?
A: Darn it!

Q: Why do worms taste like chewing gum?
A: Because they're Wrigleys!

Q: What is life like for a wood worm?
A: Boring!

Q: What makes a glow worm glow?
A: A light meal!

Q: What do you get if you cross a worm and an elephant?
A: Very big worm holes in your garden!

Q: What did the worm say to the other when he was late home?
A: Where in earth have you been!

Q: Why are glow worms good to carry in your bag?
A: They can lighten your load!

Q: How can you tell if you are looking at a police glow worm?
A: it has a blue light!

Q: What did the woodworm say to the chair?
A: It's been nice gnawing you!

Q: What did the maggot say to another?
A: What's a nice maggot like you doing in a joint like this!

Q: What do you get if you cross a worm and a young goat?

A: A dirty kid!

Q: What do you get if you cross a glow worm with some beer?

A: Light ale!

Q: Why was the glow worm unhappy?

A: Because her children weren't that bright!

Q: What's a glowworms favorite song?

A: Wake me up before you glow-glow!

Q: How do you make a glow worm happy?

A: Cut off his tail, he'll be de-lighted!

Q: How can you tell which end of a worm is which?

A: Tickle it in the middle and see which end laughs!

Q: Why didn't the two worms get on Noah's Ark in an apple?

A: Because everyone had to go on in pairs (pears)!

Q: What did the maggot say to his friend when he got stuck in an apple?

A: Worm your way out of that one!

Q: What did the earwig say as it fell down the stairs?

A: Ear we go!

Q: What kind of wig can hear?

A: An earwig!

Q: Why don't other bugs like earwigs?

A: Because they are always earwigging their conversations!

Q: What is the definition of a caterpillar?

A: A worm in a fur coat!

Q: What does a caterpillar do on New Year's Day?

A: Turns over a new leaf!

Q: What do you get if you cross a centipede and a chicken?

A: Enough drumsticks to feed an army!

Q: Why was the centipede late?

A: Because he was playing This Little Piggy with his baby brother!

Q: What has 50 legs but can't walk?
A: Half a centipede!

Q: What is worse than an alligator with toothache?
A: A centipede with athlete's foot!

Q: Why was the centipede dropped from the insect football team?
A: He took too long to put his boots on!

Q: What goes 99-clonk, 99-clonk, 99-clonk?
A: A centipede with a wooden leg!

Q: What do you call a grasshopper with no legs?
A: A grasshover!

Q: Why was the moth so unpopular?
A: He kept picking holes in everything!

Q: What's the biggest moth in the world?
A: A mammoth!

Q: Why did the moth nibble a hole in the carpet?
A: He wanted to see the floor show!

Q: How do stones stop moths from eating your clothes?

A: Because rolling stones gather no moths!

Q: What do you get if you cross a firefly and a moth?

A: An insect who can find its way around a dark wardrobe!

Q: What insect lives on nothing?

A: A moth, because it eats holes

Q: What do insects learn at school?

A: Mothmatics!

Q: How do you make a butterfly?

A: Flick it out of the butter dish with a knife!

Q: Why are mosquitos religious?

A: They prey on you!

Q: What has 6 legs, bites, and talks in code?

A: A morse-quito!

Q: What is the most religious insect?

A: A mosque-ito!

Q: What is the difference between a mosquito and a fly?

A: Try sewing buttons on a mosquito!

Q: How do you know if you have a tough mosquito?

A: You slap him and he slaps you back!

Q: What is a mosquito's favorite sport?

A: Skin-diving!

Q: Why did the mosquito go to the dentist?

A: To improve his bite!

Q: What has antlers and sucks blood?

A: A moose-quito!

Q: What do you get if you cross the Lone Ranger with an insect?

A: The Masked-quito!

Q: What did one firefly say to the other?

A: Got to glow now!

Q: If there are 5 flies in the kitchen how do you know which one is the American Football player?

A: The one in the sugar bowl!

Q: Why were the flies playing football in saucer?

A: They were playing for the cup!

Q: Which insect makes films?
A: Steven Spielbug!

Q: What goes snap, crackle, and pop?
A: A firefly with a short circuit!

Q: What insect runs away from everything?
A: A flee (flea)!

Q: What is the most faithful insect?
A: A flea, once they find someone they like they stick to them!

Q: What is a flea's favorite book?
A: The itch-hikers guide to the galaxy!

Q: What did one flea say to the other after a night out?
A: Shall we walk home or take a dog?

Q: Who rode a dog and was a confederate general during the American Civil War?
A: Robert E Flea!

Q: How do you find where a flea has bitten you?

A: Start from scratch!

Q: What to you call a Russian flea?

A: A Moscow-ito!

Q: What is the difference between a flea and a wolf?

A: One prowls on the hairy and the other howls on the prairie!

Q: How do you start an insect race?

A: One, two, flea – go!

Q: What kind of bee can keep an aeroplane dry?

A: An aero-drone!

Q: What do you get if you cross a rabbit and a flea?

A: Bugs Bunny!

Q: What does a bee say before it stings you?

A: This is going to hurt me a lot more than it hurts you!

Q: Why did the queen bee kick out all of the other bees?

A: Because they kept droning on and on!

Q: What do bees chew?
A: Bumble gum!

Q: Where do bees go on holiday?
A: Stingapore!

Q: Why do bees have sticky hair?
A: Because of the honey combs!

Q: Why did the bees go on strike?
A: Because they wanted more honey and shorter working flowers!

Q: What does the Santa Claus bee say?
A: Ho hum hum!

Q: How many bees do you need in a bee choir?
A: A humdred!

Q: What do you get if you cross a bee with a door bell?
A: A hum dinger!

Q: What's a bee's favorite novel?
A: The Great Gats-bee!

Q: What TV station do bees watch?
A: Bee bee C (BBC)!

Q: Where do bees keep their money?
A: In a honey box!

Q: What did the bee say to the other bee in summer?
A: Swarm here isn't it?

Q: Who is the bee's favorite singer?
A: Sting!

Q: Who is the bee's favorite pop group?
A: The bee gees!

Q: What is the bee's favorite film?
A: The Sting!

Q: What is a baby bee?
A: A little humbug!

Q: Who is a bee's favorite painter?
A: Pablo Beecasso!

Q: What did the spider say to the bee?
A: Your honey or your life!

Q: What does a bee get at McDonalds?
A: A humburger!

Q: Why do bees buzz?
A: Because they can't whistle!

Q: What kind of bee can't be understood?
A: A mumble bee!

Q: What goes zzub, zzub?
A: A bee flying backwards!

Q: What are the smartest bees?
A: Spelling bees!

Q: What bee is good for your health?
A: Vitamin bee!

Q: What is black and yellow and buzzes along at 30,000 feet?
A: A bee is an aeroplane!

Q: What's a bee's favorite flower?
A: bee-gonias!

Q: What did the confused bee say?
A: To bee or not to bee!

Q: What kinds of bees hum and drop things?
A: A fumble bee!

Q: What did the bee say to the flower?
A: Hello honey!

Q: Why do bees hum?
A: Because they've forgotten the words!

Q: What buzzes, is black and yellow, and goes along the bottom of the sea?
A: A bee in a submarine!

Q: Can bees fly in the rain?
A: Not without their little yellow jackets!

Q: How do we know that insects are so clever?
A: Because they always know when you're eating outside!

Q: What is the wasp's favorite song?
A: Just a Spoonful of Sugar.

Q: Where do you take a sick wasp?
A: To waspital.

Q: What are ants called when they run away very fast to get married?
A: Ant-elopers.

Q: What do you call a stupid ant?
A: Antwerp.

Q: What do you call a scruffy, lazy ant?
A: Decadent.

Q: What do you call an ant with frog's legs?
A: An antphibian.

Q: Why don't anteaters get sick?
A: Because they're full of anti-bodies!

Q: What did one mosquito say to another when they came out of the cinema?
A: Fancy a bite?

Q: Why are mosquitoes annoying?
A: Because they get under your skin.

Q: Why is it best to be bitten quickly by one mosquito?
A: Because an itch in time saves nine.

Q: What do you call A Tale of Two Mosquitoes?

A: A bite-time story.

Q: Why was the ladybird kicked out of the forest?

A: Because she was a litter bug.

Q: Which fly captured the ladybird?

A: The dragon-fly.

Q: How do you make a moth bawl?

A: Hit him with a fly swatter.

Q: If a flea and a fly pass each other what time is it?

A: Fly past flea.

Q: Why did the stupid boy wear a turtle neck sweater?

A: To hide his flea collar.

Q: What did the idiot do to the flea in his ear?

A: Shot it!

Q: Two mosquitoes were buzzing round when they saw a drunken man.

A: One said to the other, you bite him? I'm driving.

Q: What do you get if you cross a moth with a firefly?

A: An insect that can find its way around a dark closet.

Q: How do fireflies start a race?
A: Ready, steady, glow!

Cat Jokes

Q: What do you call a cat when he first wakes up with the alarm clock?
A: Catsup!

Q: Why do cats eat fur balls?
A: Because they love a good gag!

Q: What do you call it when a cat stops?
A: A paws!

Q: Why did the mother cat put stamps on her kittens?
A: Because she wanted to mail a litter.

Q: How do cats buy things?
A: From a cat-alogue!

Q: What kind of cats lay around the house?
A: Car-pets!

Q: What kind of work does a weak cat do?
A: Light mouse work.

Q: What's a cat's second favorite food?
A: Spa-catti!

Q: What's a cat's favorite food?
A: Petatoes!

Q: Which game did the cat want to play with the mouse?
A: Catch.

Q: What do you call a cat that's joined the Red Cross?
A: A first-aid kit!

Q: What do you call a cat that eats lemons?
A: A sourpuss!

Q: Why does everyone love cats?
A: They're purr-fect!

Q: Where do cats write down notes?
A: Scratch Paper!

Q: What's every cat's favorite song?
A: Three Blind Mice!

Q: Why do cats like to hear other cats make noise?
A: It's meow-sic to their ears!

Q: What did the female cat say to the male cat?

A: You're a purr-fect cat for me!

Q: What do you call it when a cat bites?
A: Catnip!

Q: What do cats like to eat on a hot day?
A: Mice cream

Q: What do you call the loser in a hissing, scratching cat fight?
A: Claude

Q: What has one horn and gives milk?
A: A milk truck.

Q: When you call a dog, they usually come to you.
A: When you call a cat; they take a message.

Q: Why couldn't the cat speak?
A: The dog taped his mouth.

Q: If a cat won an Oscar, what would he get?
A: An a-CAT-emy award.

Q: Why was the cat afraid of the tree?
A: Because of the tree bark.

Q: What is an octopus?
A: An eight-sided cat.

Q: What is another way to describe a cat?
A: A heat seeking missile!

Q: Why was the cat so small?
A: Because it only had condensed milk!

Q: When the cats away..?
A: The house smells better!

Q: Which big cat should you never play cards with?
A: A cheetah!

Q: Why are cats such good singers?
A: They're very mewsical.

Q: What do you call a cat that can spring up a six-foot wall?
A: A good jumpurr!

Q: What's furry, has whiskers, and chases outlaws?
A: A posse cat!

Q: What is a cat's favorite TV show?
A: Miami Mice!

Q: What did the cat say to the fish?
A: I've got a bone to pick with you!

Q: Why do cats never shave?
A: Because 8 out of 10 cats prefer whiskas!

Q: When is it unlucky to see a black cat?
A: When you're a mouse!

Q: Why did the cat sleep under the car?
A: Because she wanted to wake up oily!

Q: What happened when the cat swallowed a coin?
A: There was some money in the kitty!

Q: What did the cat do when he swallowed some cheese?
A: He waited by the mouse hole with baited breath!

Q: What does a cat call a bowl of mice?
A: A purrfect meal!

Q: What do you call a cat wearing boots?
A: Puss in boots!

Q: What works in a circus, walks a tightrope, and has claws?

A: An acrocat!

Q: Why did the cat put the letter M into the fridge?

A: Because it turns ice into mice!

Q: What cat purrs more than any other?

A: Purrsians!

Q: On what should you mount a statue of your cat?

A: A caterpillar!

Q: What do cats read in the morning?

A: Mewspapers!

Q: Why do cats chase birds?

A: For a lark!

Q: What kind of cat should you take into the desert?

A: A first aid kitty!

Q: What do you call a cat that has just eaten a whole duck?

A: A duck filled fatty puss!

Q: Why is a crazy marmalade cat like a biscuit?

A: They are both ginger nuts!

Q: Why do tomcats fight?

A: Because they like raising a stink!

Q: What is white, sugary, has whiskers, and floats on the sea?

A: A catameringue!

Q: There were four cats in a boat, one jumped out. How many were left?

A: None. They were all copy cats!

Q: What do you get if you cross a cat with Santa?

A: Santa Claws!

Q: How do you know that cats are not sensitive creatures?

A: They never cry over spilt milk!

Q: What is cleverer than a talking cat?

A: A spelling bee!

Q: Who was the most powerful cat in China?

A: Chairman Miaow!

Q: What do you get if you cross a cat with a tree?

A: A cat-a-logue!

Q: What's the unluckiest kind of cat to have?

A: A catastrophe!

Q: What noise does a cat make going down the highway?

A: Miaoooooooooooooooooooooooooow!

Q: How is cat food sold?

A: Usually purr can!

Q: What is the cat's favorite TV show?

A: The evening mews!

Q: What do you get if you cross a cat and a gorilla?

A: An animal that puts you out a night!

Q: How do you know if your cat has eaten a duckling?

A: She's got that down in the mouth look!

Q: How do you know if you cats got a bad cold?

A: He has cat-arrh!

Q: What did the cat say when he lost all his money?

A: I'm paw!

Q: How do cats eat spaghetti?

A: The same as everyone else - they put it in their mouths!

Q: What do you get if you cross a cat with a parrot?

A: A carrot!

Q: What happened when the cat ate a ball of wool?

A: She had mittens!

Q: What looks like half a cat?

A: The other half!

Cow Jokes

Q: What does a cow make when the sun comes out?
A: A shadow.

Q: What do you get when a cow goes to the beach with tanning oil?
A: Pre-tanned leather.

Q: What do you get if you cross a cow with an octopus?
A: A cow that can milk itself!

Q: Why do cows like being told jokes?
A: Because they like being amooooosed!

Q: What's the best way to make a bull sweat?
A: Put him in a tight jumper!

Q: If you had fifteen cows and five goats what would you have?
A: Plenty of milk!

Q: What is a cow's favorite TV show?
A: Dr. Moo!

Q: Why wouldn't anyone play with the little longhorn?

A: He was too much of a bully!

Q: Why was the calf afraid?

A: He was a cow-herd!

Q: Why was the woman arrested on a cattle ranch for wearing a silk dress?

A: She was charged with rustling!

Q: Why don't cows ever have any money?

A: Because the farmers milk them dry!

Q: Why doesn't Sweden export its cattle?

A: It wants to keep its Stockholm!

Q: Why do cows think cooks are mean?

A: They whip cream!

Q: Why did the moron give the sleepy cow a hammer?

A: He wanted her to hit the hay!

Q: Why did the farmer put his cow on the scales?

A: He wanted to see how much the milky weighed!

Q: Why did the farmer put brandy in the cow's food?

A: He wanted to raise stewed beef!

Q: Why did the farmer fence in the bull?

A: The farmer had too much of a steak in him to let him go!

Q: Why did the farmer feed money to his cow?

A: He wanted rich milk!

Q: Why did the cow jump over the moon?

A: To get to the Milky Way!

Q: Why did Bossy slug Roy Rogers?

A: She heard he was a cowpuncher!

Q: Why did Bossy tell the cowpoke to leave her calf alone?

A: She thought children should be seen and not herded!

Q: Why couldn't the cow leave the farm?

A: She was pasteurized!

Q: Why are cows made for dancing?

A: They're all born hoofers!

Q: Where does a cow stop to drink?
A: The Milky Way!

Q: Where do steers go to dance?
A: To the Meat Ball!

Q: Where do Russian cows come from?
A: Moscow!

Q: Where do milk shakes come from?
A: Nervous cows!

Q: Where do Danish cows come from?
A: Cowpenhagen

Q: Where do cows like to ride on trains?
A: In the cow-boose.

Q: Where do cows like to live?
A: St. Moo-is.

Q: Where do baby cows eat?
A: To the calf-ateria!

Q: Where did the bull carry his stock-market report?
A: In his beef case!

Q: When is a farmer like a magician?
A: When he turns his cow into pasture.

Q: When a bull wants to listen to a cassette, what does he put on his head?
A: Steer phones!

Q: What's a cow's favorite moosical note?
A: Beef-flat!

Q: What would you hear at a cow concert?
A: Moo-sic!

Q: What would you get if you crossed a cow with a rabbit?
A: Hare in your milk!

Q: What U.S. state has the most cows?
A: Moosouri!

Q: What two members of the cow family go everywhere with you?
A: Your calves!

Q: What South American dance do cows like to do?
A: The Rump-a

Q: What sound do you hear when you drop a bomb on a cow?
A: Cowboom!

Q: What newspaper do cows read?
A: The Daily Moos.

Q: What magazine makes cows stampede to the newsstand?
A: Cows-mopolitan!

Q: What kind of cows do you find in Alaska?
A: Eski-moos!

Q: What is the most important use for cowhide?
A: To hold the cow together.

Q: What is the golden rule for cows?
A: Do unto udders as you would have udders do to you!

Q: What is the definition of moon?
A: The past tense of moo!

Q: What is the definition of derange?
A: De place where de cowboys ride!

Q: What is a cow's favorite lunchmeat?
A: Bullogna.

Q: What has four legs and goes, oom! oom!?
A: A cow walking backwards!

Q: What happens when a cow stops shaving?
A: It grows a moostache.

Q: What happens when the cows refuse to be milked?
A: Udder chaos!

Q: What hair style is a calves' favorite?
A: The cowlick!

Q: What happened to the lost cattle?
A: Nobody's herd.

Q: What gives milk and has a horn?
A: A milk tank!

Q: What goes oo ooo oooo?
A: A cow with no lips.

Q: What game do little cows like to play?
A: Moonopoly.

Q: What famous painting do cows love to look at?

A: The Moooona Lisa!

Q: What does a cow ride when his car is broken?

A: A COW-asaki MOO-torcycle!

Q: What does a cow like to do by a campfire?

A: Roast moosmallows!

Q: What do you get when you cross a cow with a kangaroo?

A: A kangamoo!

Q: What do you get if you cross Bossy with a vampire?

A: Dracowla!

Q: What do you get if you cross a steer and a chicken?

A: Roost beef!

Q: What do you get if you cross a longhorn with a knight?

A: Sir Loin!

Q: What do you get if you cross a cow, a French fry, and a sofa?

A: A cowch potato!

Q: What do you get if you cross a cow with a tension headache?

A: A bad mood!

Q: What do you get if you cross a cow with a spaniel, a poodle, and a rooster?

A: A cockerpoodlemoo!

Q: What do you get from pampered cows?
A: Spoiled milk!

Q: What do you get from an invisible cow?
A: Evaporated milk!

Q: What do you get from a short-legged cow?

A: Dragon milk!

Q: What do you get from a forgetful cow?
A: Milk of amnesia!

Q: What do you get from a cowmedian?
A: Cream of wit!

Q: What do you get from a cow on the North Pole?
A: Cold cream!

Q: What do you call it when one bull spies on another bull?
A: A steak-out!

Q: What do you call it when cows do battle in outer space?
A: Steer Wars.

Q: What do you call explosive cow vomit?
A: A cud missile!

Q: What do you call a herd of cows in a psychiatrist's office?
A: An encownter group.

Q: What do you call a cow who works for a gardener?
A: A lawn moo-er.

Q: What do you call a cow that's just had a baby?
A: De-calfinated!

Q: What do you call a cow that fell in a hole?
A: A hole-y cow!

Q: What do you call a tired cow?
A: Milked out!

Q: What do you call a cow that doesn't give milk?
A: A milk dud!

Q: What do you call a sleeping bull?
A: A bull-dozer.

Q: What do you call a group of cattle sent into orbit?
A: The first herd shot round the world!

Q: What do you call a cow with no front legs?
A: Lean Beef

Q: What do you call a cow who argues with her husband?
A: A bullfighter!

Q: What do you call a cow on the barnyard floor?
A: Ground beef.

Q: What do you call a bull that's sent overseas by boat?

A: Shipped beef!

Q: What do you call a bull that runs into a threshing machine?

A: Hamburger!

Q: What do cows usually fly around in?

A: Helicowpters and bulloons.

Q: What do cows wear when they're vacationing in Hawaii?

A: Moo moos.

Q: What do cows sing at their friend's birthday parties?

A: Happy birthday to MOO, Happy Birthday to MOO.

Q: What do cows read at the breakfast table?

A: The moospaper!

Q: What do cows like to listen to?

A: Moo-sic!

Q: What do cows like to do at amoosement parks?

A: Ride on the roller cowster.

Q: What do cows get when they do all their chores?

A: Mooney.

Q: What do cows get when they are sick?

A: Hay Fever.

Q: What do cows do when there introduced?

A: They give each other a milk shake!

Q: What do cows do for entertainment?

A: They go to the moooovies.

Q: What do cows call Frank Sinatra?

A: Old Moo Eyes!

Q: What did the moron say when he saw the milk cartons in the grass?

A: Hey! Look at the cows nest!

Q: What did the cow wear to the football game?

A: A jersey.

Q: What did the calf say to the silo?
A: Is my fodder in there?

Q: What did one dairy cow say to another?
A: Got milk?

Q: What country do cows love to visit?
A: Moo Zealand!

Q: What band is a cow favorite?
A: Moody Blues.

Q: What are the spots on black-and-white cows?
A: Holstaines.

Q: What are cow's favorite party games?
A: MOO-sical chairs!

Q: What animals do you bring to bed?
A: Your calves.

Q: That tornado damage your cow barn any?
A: Not sure. Haven't found the darn thing yet!

Q: That bull you sold me is a lazy good-for-nothing!

A: I told you he was a bum steer!

Q: How to you know that cows will be in heaven?

A: It's a place of udder delight.

Q: How does a cow do math?

A: With a cowculator!

Q: How do you make a milkshake?

A: Give a cow a pogo stick.

Q: How do bulls drive their cars?

A: They steer them!

Q: How did the farmer find his lost cow?

A: He tractor down.

Q: What do you call a cow that plays the guitar?

A: A moosician!

Q: How did the calf's final exam turn out?

A: Grade A!

Q: How did that bullfight come out?

A: Oh, it was a toss-up!

Q: How did cows feel when the branding iron was invented?

A: They were very impressed!

Q: Does running out of a burning barn make a cow unusual?

A: No, only medium rare!

Q: Did you hear about the snobby cow?

A: She thought she was a cutlet above the rest!

Q: Did you hear about the farmer who lost control of his tractor in the cow pasture?

A: No!

Q: Did he hurt the cows?

A: No, he just grazed them!

Q: I've just discovered a method for making wool out of milk!

A: But doesn't that make the cow feel a little sheepish?

Q: Is there big money in the cattle business?

A: So I've herd!

Q: In what state will you find the most cows?

A: Moo York!

Q: If you make a cow angry, how will she get even?

A: She'll cream you!

Q: If you crossed two cows with a flock of ducks, what would you get?

A: Milk and quackers!

Q: If you crossed a cow with Michael Jackson, what song would you get?

A: Beef it!

Q: If you crossed a cow with a goat, what would you get?

A: Half and half!

Q: What advice do cows give?

A: Turn the udder cheek and mooooove on!

Dog Jokes

Q: Why does a dog wag its tail?
A: No one else will do it for them

Q: What side of the dog has the most fur?
A: The Outside.

Q: What goes krab, krab, krab?
A: A dog barking in a mirror.

Q: What did the puppy say when he sat on sandpaper?
A: RUFF!

Q: What kind of dog does Dracula like?
A: A Bloodhound.

Q: Why did the lazy person buy a tall dog?
A: So that they didn't have to bend down to pet it.

Q: What happened when the dog went to the flea circus?
A: It stole the show!

Q: When is a strange dog most likely to go into your house?

A: When the door is open.

Q: Why is a dog's nose in the middle of its face?

A: Because it's the scenter.

Q: Why did the dog cross the road?

A: Because it was the chicken's day off.

Q: What do you say to a dog before he eats?

A: Bone appetite!

Q: How do you get a dog to stop barking in the back seat of a car?

A: Put him in the front seat.

Q: What has four legs and an arm?

A: A Rottweiler in a playground.

Q: How did bulldogs get such flat noses?

A: From chasing cars.

Q: Why do dogs bury bones in the ground?

A: Because you can't bury them in the sky!

Q: When's the best time to take your Doberman pinscher for a walk?
A: Anytime he wants to go.

Q: Why is a dog with a lame leg like adding 6 and 7s?
A: He puts down the three and carries the one.

Q: Would you rather have a 300-pound dog chase you or a tiger?
A: I'd rather have him chase the tiger.

Q: Why was the mother flea so unhappy?
A: All her children have gone to the dogs.

Q: Why is a dog so warm in summer?
A: He wears a coat and pants.

Q: Why is a dog like a baseball player?
A: He runs for home when he sees the catcher coming.

Q: Why doesn't a dog ever have a nose 12 inches long?
A: Because then it would be a foot.

Q: Why does a dog scratch himself?

A: He is the only one that knows where it itches.

Q: Why do dogs turn around three times before lying down?

A: One good turn deserves another.

Q: Why didn't the dog play cards on his ocean cruise?

A: Because the captain stood on the deck.

Q: Why did the thoughtful father buy his six children a dachshund?

A: He wanted a dog they could all pet at once.

Q: Why did the dog's owner think his dog was a great mathematician?

A: When he asked the dog what six minus six was, the dog said nothing.

Q: Why did the dog sleep so poorly?

A: By mistake he plugged his electric blanket into the toaster and kept popping out of bed all night!

Q: Why did the dog say he was an actor?
A: His leg was in a cast.

Q: Why did the dog run in circles?
A: He was a watchdog and needed winding.

Q: Why did the dog mistake the dog catcher for a grape?
A: He was color-blind.

Q: Why did the dog go to the doctor after a tomato fell on his head?
A: The tomato was in a can.

Q: Which dog tastes better when eaten?
A: A hot dog.

Q: Which dog is always without a tail?
A: A hot dog.

Q: Which dog looks like a cat?
A: A police dog in disguise.

Q: Which dog eats with its tail?
A: All dogs keep their tails on when eating.

Q: Which dog can tell time?
A: A watchdog.

Q: Where do you usually find dogs?
A: It all depends on where you lose them.

Q: When you catch your dog eating a dictionary, what should you do?

A: Take the words right out of his mouth.

Q: When is a dog most impolite?

A: When he points.

Q: What would you call a nine day old dog in Russia?

A: A puppy.

Q: What would you get if you crossed a chicken with a dog?

A: A hen that lays pooched eggs.

Q: What was the dog doing on the turnpike?

A: About seven miles an hour.

Q: What should you know before you teach your dog a new trick?

A: You should know more than your dog.

Q: What should you do if you see a vicious dog?

A: Hope he doesn't see you.

Q: What should you do if you find an angry 500-pound dog in your kitchen?
A: Go out to eat.

Q: What place of business helps dogs who have lost their tails?
A: A retail store.

Q: What looks like a dog, sounds like a dog, eats like a dog, but isn't a dog?
A: A pup.

Q: What is worse than a dog howling at the moon?
A: Two dogs howling at the moon.

Q: What is the difference between a dog and a mailbox?
A: If you don't know you must lose a lot of mail.

Q: What is the difference between a barking dog and an umbrella?
A: The umbrella can be shut up.

Q: What is taller when it sits down than when it stands up?
A: A dog.

Q: What is black and white and red all over?

A: A Dalmatian with bad sunburn.

Q: What is a dog who crosses the street twice in an hour?

A: A double crosser.

Q: What has 2,000 eyes and 4,000 feet?

A: A thousand dogs.

Q: What is a baseball dog?

A: One that chases fowls.

Q: What happened when the shaggy dog swallowed a teaspoon?

A: He wasn't able to stir.

Q: What happened to the dog that fell into a lens-grinding machine?

A: He made a spectacle of himself.

Q: What did the dog use to make his kite?

A: Flypaper.

Q: What did the dog take when he was run down?

A: The license number of the car that hit him.

Q: What did the dog say to the pig?

A: You are just a boar.

Q: What did the dog say when he chased his tail?

A: This is the end.

Q: What did the dog get when he multiplied 497 by 684?

A: The wrong answer.

Q: What did the dog do with the history professor?

A: They got together and talked about old times.

Q: What did the dog do when the panhandler put the bite on him?

A: Bit him, naturally.

Q: How do you keep a dog from barking in your front yard?

A: Put him in your back yard.

Q: How did the dog's owner know his pet was angry about having soap flakes for breakfast?

A: He foamed at the mouth.

Q: How did the dog make anti-freeze?
A: He stole her blanket.

Q: How did the dog make gold soup?
A: He put in 24 carrots.

Q: How did the dog get into the locked cemetery at night?
A: He used a skeleton key.

Q: How did the dog feel when he lost his flashlight?
A: Delighted.

Q: How can you tell a dog from an elephant?
A: The elephant remembers.

Q: How can you tell a dog from a tomato?
A: The tomato is red.

Q: How do you find your dog if he's lost in the woods?
A: Put your ear up to a tree and listen for the bark!

Q: Why do dogs run in circles?
A: Because it's hard to run in squares!

Q: Why did the dog have a gleam in his eye?

A: Someone bumped his elbow while he was brushing his teeth.

Q: What do you call a black Eskimo dog?

A: A dusky husky!

Q: What do you call a sheepdog's tail that can tell tall stories?

A: A shaggy dog's tale!

Q: How do you feel if you cross a sheepdog with a melon?

A: Melon-collie!

Q: What do you call a dog with no legs?

A: It doesn't matter what you call him he still won't come!

Q: What do you call a litter of young dogs that have come in from the snow?

A: Slush puppies!

Q: What do you get if you cross a dog with a frog?

A: A dog that can lick you from the other side of the road!

Q: What do you get if cross two young dogs with a pair of earplugs?

A: Hush puppies!

Q: What do you get if you cross a dog and a sheep?

A: A sheep that can round itself up!

Q: What do you get if you cross a dog with a kangaroo?

A: A dog that has somewhere to put its own lead!

Q: What do you get if you cross a computer and a Rottweiler?

A: A computer with a lot of bites!

Q: What happens to a dog that keeps eating bits off of the table?

A: He gets splinters in his mouth!

Q: What do you get if you cross a Beatle and an Australian dog?

A: Dingo Starr!

Q: What do you get if you cross a dog with a blind mole?

A: A dog that keeps barking up the wrong tree!

Q: When is a black dog not a black dog?
A: When it's a greyhound!

Q: What do you call a dog in the middle of a muddy road?
A: A mutt in a rut!

Q: Why do you need a license for a dog and not for a cat?
A: Cats can't drive!

Q: What do you get if you cross a sheepdog with a jelly?
A: The collie wobbles!

Q: What do you call a dog in jeans and a sweater?
A: A plain clothes police dog!

Q: What kind of dog wears a uniform and medals?
A: A guard dog!

Q: What kind of dog chases anything red?
A: A bull dog!

Q: When does a dog go moo?
A: When it is learning a new language!

Q: How do you stop a dog from smelling?
A: Put a peg on its nose!

Q: Why is it called a litter of puppies?
A: Because they mess up the whole house!

Q: What's a dog's favorite hobby?
A: Collecting fleas!

Q: How many seasons are there in a dog's life?
A: Just one, the molting season!

Q: What is a dog's favorite flower?
A: Anything in your garden!

Q: What dog wears contact lenses?
A: A cock-eyed spaniel!

Q: What is a dog's favorite food?
A: Anything that is on your plate!

Q: What is a dog's favorite sport?
A: Formula 1 drooling!

Q: What do you call an alcoholic dog?
A: A whino!

Q: What do dogs have that no other animal has?

A: Puppy dogs!

Q: What do you get if you cross a Rottweiler and a hyena?

A: I don't know, but I'll join in if it laughs!

Q: What did the hungry Dalmatian say when he had a meal?

A: That hit the spots!

Q: What kind of dog sounds like you can eat it?

A: A sausage dog!

Q: What do you get if you cross a dog and a cheetah?

A: A dog that chases cars - and catches them!

Q: What is the difference between Father Christmas and a warm dog?

A: Father Christmas wears a whole suit; a dog just wears pants!

Q: Where do Eskimos train their dogs?

A: In the mush room!

Q: What do you get if you cross a giraffe with a dog?

A: An animal that barks at low flying aircraft!

Q: Why did the dog wear white sneakers?

A: Because his boots were at the menders!

Q: What do you get if you cross a dog with Concorde?

A: A jet setter!

Q: What happened to the dog that ate nothing but garlic?

A: His bark was much worse than his bite!

Q: What did the angry man sing when he found his slippers chewed up by the new puppy?

A: I must throw that doggie out the window!

Q: What sort of clothes does a pet dog wear?

A: A petticoat!

Q: What do you get if you cross a sheepdog with a rose?

A: A collie-flower!

Q: What kind of meat do you give a stupid dog?

A: Chump chops!

Q: What do you get if you take a really big dog out for a walk?

A: A Great Dane out!

Q: What did the cowboy say when the bear ate Lassie?

A: Well, doggone!

Q: Who is the dog's favorite comedian?

A: Groucho Marx!

Q: What is the dog's favorite city?

A: New Yorkie!

Q: Why didn't the dog speak to his foot?

A: Because its not polite to talk back to your paw!

Q: What kind of dog sniffs out new flowers?

A: A bud hound!

Q: What do you call a nutty dog in Australia?

A: A dingo-ling!

Q: What do you call a happy Lassie?
A: A jolly collie!

Q: Where did the dog breeder keep his savings?
A: In bark-lays bank!

Q: What does a Chihuahua play basketball with?
A: A tennis ball!

Q: What kinds of computers do Chihuahuas like best?
A: Lap-top!

Q: How are you going to pay the Chihuahua who helped you to set up your computer?
A: With dog diskettes!

Q: Why is it hard for Chihuahuas to type on a keyboard?
A: They're all paws.

Q: What kind of dog is a person's best friend?
A: A palmatian!

Q: What do you call a boring dog?
A: A dull-mation!

Q: Dad, I spotted a Dalmatian!
A: No need to, it already has its own spots!

Q: What dog is cousin to the Dalmatian?
A: A spot-weiler!

Q: What is brown and gray, has eight legs, and is carrying a large trunk and a small trunk?
A: A Chihuahua on vacation with an elephant.

Q: Why should you never watch a video with a Chihuahua?
A: It always plays with the paws button on the VCR.

Q: What kind of leash should you buy for a Chihuahua?
A: A short one!

Q: What is a Chihuahua's favorite sport?
A: Miniature golf!

Q: Why are Chihuahuas such good bedtime storytellers?
A: They have short tales!

Q: Where will a springer spaniel never shop?

A: At a flea market!

Q: What is your dog's favorite breakfast?

A: Pooched eggs!

Q: How do you make a dog float?

A: Take two scoops of ice cream, a couple of squirts of soda, and a small dog.

Q: If a beagle can't play a bugle in the marching band, what's his other favorite instrument to play?

A: A trombone.

Q: What should you do if you have a basset hound over for dinner?

A: Have a short table!

Q: What dog sweats the most and drinks the most water?

A: A hot-weiler!

Q: How can you make a basset hound fast?

A: Take away its food!

Q: What dogs never gets lost?

A: Newfound-lands!

Q: When are Pomeranians good at taking photographs?
A: Only when they snap at something!

Q: What dog always gets on everyone's nerves?
A: A great pane!

Q: What dog takes the money and runs fast!
A: A payhound!

Q: What dog do other dogs tell their problems to?
A: A complaint Bernard!

Q: What kind of dog is the smartest?
A: A great brain!

Q: What dog would you want on your American football team?
A: A golden receiver!

Q: How did the little Scottish dog feel when he saw a monster?
A: Terrier-fied!

Q: What dog do other dogs go to when they are sick?

A: A docs-hund!

Q: What do you get when you cross a collie with a trumpet?

A: A Lassie who plays brassie!

Q: What is the best kind of dog to direct traffic at a busy intersection?

A: A pointer!

Q: What kind of dog doesn't do well in hot weather?

A: A faint Bernard!

Q: What do you get when you cross a sled dog with an elephant?

A: A tusky!

Q: What kind of dog can tell time?

A: A clockshund!

Q: What dog wears a white coat and does science experiments?

A: Labs!

Q: What kind of dog always needs a shave?

A: A bearded collie!

Q: What wears a black, white, and tan coat but has no hair?
A: A bald beagle!

Q: What kind of dog is the most colorful?
A: A paint Bernard!

Q: What dog is always tired in London?
A: An English sleep dog.

Q: What dogs are best for sending telegrams?
A: Wire haired terriers!

Q: What kind of dog can you best see in the dark?
A: A glowberman pinscher!

Q: What is a collie puppy's favorite toy?
A: A chew-chew train!

Q: What has eighteen legs and fetches a ball?
A: The Philadelphia Beagles!

Q: What is the only breed of dog a boxer is afraid of?
A: A Doberman puncher!

Q: What is the best kind of dog to ask for directions?

A: A Chihuahua, because it knows all the shortcuts!

Q: Where do you take a Chihuahua that has fallen into a lake?

A: To a weterinarian!

Q: What do you do when a Chihuahua sneezes?

A: Get a small hankie!

Q: What kind of pants do you buy for your pet Chihuahua?

A: Shorts!

Q: What is black and white and red all over?

A: A Chihuahua in a tuxedo that tripped into a jar of salsa!

Q: Why can't Chihuahuas run marathons?

A: They're short of breath!

Q: What did the elephant say when it saw the Chihuahuas coming down the road?

A: Look out for the mice!

Q: Why do Chihuahuas have such short necks?

A: Because their heads are so close to their bodies!

Q: How did the Chihuahua disappear on the road?

A: It was using a hide-n-go-seekle!

Q: Why did the dog jump into the sea?

A: He wanted to chase the catfish!

Q: What do you get if you cross a Labrador and a tortoise?

A: A dog that will run to the shop to get your paper and bring back last week's paper!

Q: What do you get when you cross a Doberman with a bird?

A: A Doberman fincher!

Q: What dog rides a horse named Macaroni?

A: Yankee poodle!

Q: What is the best way to follow a lost dogs paw prints?

A: With a track-tor!

Q: When George Washington was a general, why did he like to have dogs around?

A: They were very helpful during the Roverlutionary War!

Q: What sort of clothes does a pet dog wear?

A: A petticoat!

Q: What kind of modeling clay does a dog use?

A: Fi-Do!

Q: How many hairs are in a dog's tail?

A: None. They are all on the outside.

Q: Why did the 3-legged dog go back to Dodge City?

A: To see who shot his paw.

Q: What game do 18 dogs like to play during the summer?

A: Woofleball.

Q: Why is a dog scared of a fire?

A: It doesn't want to become a hot dog.

Elephant Jokes

Q: What happened when the elephant sat on the car?
A: Everyone knows a Mercedes bends!

Q: Why did the elephant eat the candle?
A: He wanted a light snack!

Q: Two elephants jumped off a cliff...
A: BOOM BOOM!

Q: Why do elephants do well in school?
A: Because they have a lot of grey matter!

Q: What do you call an elephant that can't do math?
A: Dumbo!

Q: How do you know that peanuts are fattening?
A: Have you ever seen a skinny elephant?

Q: When should you feed milk to a baby elephant?
A: When it's a baby elephant!

Q: Why did the elephant eat the candle?
A: For light refreshment!

Q: Have you heard about the elephant that went on a crash diet?
A: He wrecked three cars, a bus, and two fire engines!

Q: Why do elephants eat raw food?
A: Because they don't know how to cook!

Q: Why are elephants wiser than chickens?
A: Have you ever heard of Kentucky Fried Elephant?!

Q: How can you tell if there is an elephant in your dessert?
A: You get very lumpy ice cream!

Q: What did the grape say when the elephant stood on it?
A: Nothing, it just let out a little wine!

Q: How do you get an elephant into a matchbox?
A: Take all the matches out first!

Q: What did the hotel manager say to the elephant that couldn't pay his bill?

A: Pack your trunk and clear out!

Q: Why did the elephant cross the road?

A: Because the chicken was having a day off!

Q: How does an elephant get out of a small car?

A: The same way that he got in!

Q: How do you fit five elephants into a car?

A: Two in the front, two in the back and the other in the glove compartment!

Q: Why do elephants have trunks?

A: Because they would look silly carrying suitcases!

Q: What kind of elephant lives in Antarctica?

A: Cold ones!

Q: What pill would you give to an elephant that can't sleep?

A: Trunkquilizers!

Q: What's the difference between an elephant and a gooseberry?

A: A gooseberry is green!

Q: What's the difference between an African elephant and an Indian elephant?

A: About 3,000 miles!

Q: Why are elephants grey?

A: So you can tell them apart from flamingos!

Q: What's the difference between an elephant and a banana?

A: Have you ever tried to peel an elephant?

Q: What's the difference between a sick elephant and seven days?

A: One is a weak one and the other one week!

Q: What's the difference between an elephant and a piece of paper?

A: You can't make a paper airplane out of an elephant!

Q: How do you tell the difference between an elephant and a mouse?

A: Try picking them up!

Q: What's the difference between an elephant and a bad pupil?
A: One rarely bites and the other barely writes!

Q: What's the difference between an injured elephant and bad weather?
A: One roars with pain and the other pours with rain!

Q: What's grey, beautiful and wears glass slippers?
A: Cinderelephant!

Q: What's grey, has a wand, huge wings, and gives money to elephants?
A: The tusk fairy!

Q: What's grey, carries a bunch of flowers and cheers you up when you're ill?
A: A get wellephant!

Q: What's grey but turns red?
A: An embarrassed elephant!

Q: What's grey and lights up?
A: An electric elephant!

Q: What's as big as an elephant but weighs nothing?

A: An elephant's shadow!

Q: What has 3 tails, 4 trunks and 6 feet?

A: An elephant with spare parts!

Q: What goes up slowly and comes down quickly?

A: An elephant in a lift!

Q: What's grey and wrinkly and jumps every twenty seconds?

A: An elephant with hiccups!

Q: What's blue and has big ears?

A: An elephant at the North Pole!

Q: What weighs 4 tons and is bright red?

A: An elephant holding its breath!

Q: What's big, grey and flies straight up?

A: An elecopter!

Q: What's big and grey and protects you from the rain?

A: An umbrellaphant!

Q: What's yellow on the outside and grey on the inside?

A: An elephant disguised as a banana!

Q: What's big and grey and lives in a lake in Scotland?

A: The Loch Ness Elephant!

Q: What's grey and goes round and round?

A: An elephant in a washing machine!

Q: What's grey and never needs ironing?

A: A drip dry elephant!

Q: What's grey, stands in a river when it rains, and doesn't get wet?

A: An elephant with an umbrella!

Q: What's big and grey and wears a mask?

A: The elephantom of the opera!

Q: What's grey and moves at a hundred miles an hour?

A: A jet-propelled elephant!

Q: Why does an elephant wear sneakers?

A: So that he can sneak up on mice!

Q: Why were the elephants thrown out of the swimming pool?

A: Because they couldn't hold their trunks up!

Q: Why did the elephant paint himself with different colors?

A: Because he wanted to hide in the coloring box!

Q: How does an elephant get down from a tree?

A: He sits on a leaf and waits until autumn!

Q: How do you hire an elephant?

A: Stand it on four bricks!

Q: Who do elephants get their Christmas presents from?

A: Elephanta Claus!

Q: What do elephants sing at Christmas?

A: Noel-ephants, Noel-ephants!

Q: What do you get if you cross a parrot with an elephant?

A: An animal that tells you everything that it remembers!

Q: What did the elephant say when the man grabbed him by the tail?
A: This is the end of me!

Q: What is a baby elephant after he is five weeks old?
A: Six weeks old!

Q: Why did the elephant jump in the lake when it began to rain?
A: To stop getting wet!

Q: What did the elephant say to the famous detective?
A: It's ele-mentary, my dear Sherlock!

Q: What do elephants say as a compliment?
A: You look elephantastic!

Q: What is an elephant's favorite film?
A: Elephantasia!

Q: Who lost a herd of elephants?
A: Big Bo Peep!

Q: What do elephants do in the evenings?
A: Watch elevision!

Q: What do you do with old cannon balls?

A: Give them to elephants to use as marbles!

Q: What is stronger, an elephant or a snail?

A: A snail because it carries its house, an elephant just carries its trunk!

Q: What do you find in an elephant's graveyard?

A: Elephantoms!

Q: What animals were last to leave the ark?

A: The elephants because they had to pack their trunks!

Q: Why do elephants have trunks?

A: Because they have no pockets to put things in!

Q: What do you give an elephant with big feet?

A: Plenty of room!

Q: How to elephants talk to each other?
A: By elephone!

Q: What do you call the rabbit up the elephant's sweater?

A: Terrified!

Q: What do you call an elephant creeping through the jungle in the middle of the night?

A: Russell!

Q: What do you call an elephant that lays across the middle of a tennis court?

A: Annette!

Q: What do you call an elephant with a carrot in each ear?

A: Anything you want because he can't hear you!

Q: Why don't elephants like playing cards in the jungle?

A: Because of all the cheetahs!

Q: What's the best way to see a charging herd of elephants?

A: On television!

Q: What did Tarzan say when he saw the elephants coming?

A: Here come the elephants!

Q: What is an easy way to get a wild elephant?

A: Get a tame one and annoy it!

Q: Why do elephants jump across rivers?

A: So they won't step on the fish.

Q: Why do elephants squirt water through their noses?

A: If they squirted it through their tails, it'd be very difficult to aim.

Q: Why do elephants live in the jungle?

A: Because it's out of the high rent district.

Q: Why don't elephants like martinis?

A: Have you ever tried to get an olive out of your nose?

Q: Why are elephants large, grey and wrinkly?

A: Because if they were small, round and white, they would be aspirins.

Q: Why do elephants prefer peanuts to caviar?

A: Because they're easier to get at the ballpark.

Q: Why did the gum cross the road?
A: Because it was under the elephant's foot.

Q: What does a bald elephant wear for a toupee?
A: A sheep.

Q: What do you get if you cross an elephant with the abominable snowman?
A: A jumbo yeti.

Q: How does an elephant go up a tree?
A: It stands on an acorn and waits for it to grow.

Q: How do you make an elephant sandwich?
A: First of all, you get a very large loaf of bread.

Q: How do you raise a baby elephant?
A: With a fork lift truck!

Q: What is worse than raining cats and dogs?
A: Raining elephants!

Q: Why is an elephant braver than a hen?
A: Because the elephant isn't chicken!

Q: Why do elephants have short tails?

A: Because they can't remember long stories!

Q: What did the baby elephant get when the daddy elephant sneezed?

A: Out of the way!

Q: How do you stop an angry elephant from charging?

A: Take away its credit cards.

Fish Jokes

Q: What's a sea serpents favorite meal?
A: Fish and ships!

Q: What fish make the best sandwiches?
A: A peanut butter and jellyfish!

Q: What's the difference between an angler and a dunce?
A: One baits his hooks while the other hates his books.

Q: What kind of musical instrument can you use for fishing?
A: The cast-a-net.

Q: How many fishermen does it take to change a light bulb?
A: One, but you should have seen the bulb. It must have been THIS big.

Q: Where do fish wash?
A: In a river basin!

Q: Which fish can perform operations?
A: A sturgeon fish!

Q: What fish goes up the river at 100mph?
A: A motor pike!

Q: What do you get when four men go fishing and one comes back not catching anything?
A: Three men and a baby!

Q: What do you call a deaf fishing boat captain?
A: Anything you like, he can't hear you.

Q: Where do fish sleep?
A: In a riverbed!

Q: How much fishing tackle can a man accumulate before his wife throws him out?
A: I don't know the answer, but I think I'm nearly there.

Q: What is the difference between a fish and a piano?
A: You can't tuna fish.

Q: How many morons does it take to go ice fishing?
A: Four; one to cut the hole in the ice, and three to push the boat through.

Q: What do you call a man with a large flatfish on his head?
A: Ray!

Q: Why are fish no good at tennis?
A: They don't like to get too close to the net!

Q: How did the fish's tail get stuck in the anchor chain?
A: It was just a fluke!

Q: What's the best way to catch a fish?
A: Have someone throw it at you.

Q: What do you get if you cross a trout with an apartment?
A: A flat fish!

Q: How do you tune a fish?
A: With its scales!

Q: What fish sounds like a telephone?
A: Herring, herring, herring, herring, herring, herring.

Q: Where are most fish found?
A: Between the head and the tail!

Q: What kind of fish is useful in freezing weather?

A: Skate!

Q: How do you communicate with a fish?

A: You drop it a line!

Q: Why are fish so gullible?

A: They fall for things: Hook, line, and sinker!

Q: What do you call a big fish that makes you an offer you can't refuse?

A: The Codfather!

Q: What do romantic fish sing to each other?

A: Salmon-chanted evening!

Q: What was the Tsar of Russia's favorite fish?

A: Tsardines!

Q: What will Santa bring your fish this Christmas?

A: A scale letrix!

Q: Why are gold fish orange?

A: The water makes them rusty!

Q: What was the name of Tom Sawyer's fish?
A: Huckleberry Fin!

Q: Why are fish boots the warmest ones to wear?
A: Because they have electric eels!

Q: What did the fish do when his piano sounded odd?
A: He called the piano tuna!

Q: Why are fish cleverer than humans?
A: Ever seen a fish spend a fortune trying to hook a human?

Q: What kind of fish will help you hear well?
A: A herring aid!

Q: What do you get if you cross an abbot with a trout?
A: Monkfish!

Q: Which fish dresses the best?
A: The Swordfish - It always looks sharp!

Q: Where do fish come from?
A: Finland!

Q: Why do penguins eat fish?

A: Because donuts get soggy before they can catch them.

Q: Why are sardines the stupidest fish in the sea?

A: Because they climb into tins, close the lid, and leave the key outside!

Q: What did the sardine call the submarine?

A: A can of people!

Q: Why is a fish easy to weigh?

A: Because it has its own scales!

Q: Who sleeps at the bottom of the sea?

A: Jack the kipper!

Q: What is dry on the outside, filled with water, and blows up buildings?

A: A fish tank!

Q: What fish do road-menders use?

A: Pneumatic krill!

Q: What do you call a literary fish?

A: Salmon Rushdie!

Q: What part of a fish weighs the most?
A: Its scales!

Q: What TV game shows do fish like best?
A: Name that tuna!

Q: What do you get if you cross a salmon, a birds leg, and a hand?
A: Birds thigh fish fingers!

Q: What kind of money do fishermen make?
A: Net profits!

Q: What bit of fish doesn't make sense?
A: The piece of cod that passeth all understanding!

Q: Which fish go to heaven when they die?
A: Angelfish!

Q: Why are fish so smart?
A: They are always in schools!

Q: What do you call a fish with no eyes?
A: Fish!

Q: How do fish go into business?
A: The start on a small scale!

Q: When fish play football, who is the captain?
A: The teams kipper!

Q: What did Noah do while spending time on the ark?
A: Fished, but he didn't catch much. He only had two worms!

Q: What sort of net is useless for catching fish?
A: A football net!

Q: Have you seen the new fishing website?
A: No, it's not online yet.

Q: Why do men like to go fishing so much?
A: They finally found someone as smart as them to talk to.

Q: What do dirty fish read?
A: Prawno magazines!

Q: What do naked fish play with?
A: Bare-a-cudas!

Q: What fish only swims at night?
A: A starfish!

Q: To whom do fish go to borrow money?
A: The loan shark!

Q: How do the fish get to school?
A: By octobus!

Q: What do you call a dangerous fish that drinks too much?
A: A beer-a-cuda!

Q: How do you get around fast on the bottom of the sea?
A: Skates!

Q: What fish is best to have in a boat?
A: A Sailfish.

Q: What is a knight's favorite fish?
A: A swordfish!

Q: Why should you use six hooks on your fishing line?
A: eFISHancy!

Q: What kind of a fish does your parrot sit on?
A: A perch!

Q: Where do you go to meet the best fish?
A: It doesn't matter - any old place will do.

Q: How do you post a fish?
A: You send it COD or first bass mail!

Monkey Jokes

Q: How do you make a gorilla stew?
A: You keep it waiting for three hours!

Q: What happens when you throw one banana to two hungry apes?
A: A banana split!

Q: What excuse does an ape give for abducting a pretty girl?
A: I can't help it - she brings out the beast in me!

Q: What does a gorilla learn first in school?
A: The apey-cees!

Q: What does a gorilla attorney study?
A: The Law of the Jungle!

Q: What do you feed a 600 pound gorilla?
A: Anything it wants!

Q: What did the gorilla call his first wife?
A: His prime-mate!

Q: If you throw a great ape into one of the Great Lakes, what will it become?

A: Wet!

Q: How do you make a gorilla laugh?

A: Tell it an elephant joke!

Q: Why did the ape run around with a piece of raw meat on his head?

A: He thought he was a griller (gorilla)!

Q: Why do gorillas have big nostrils?

A: They have big fingers.

Q: Why do primates do so well in show biz?

A: Put any ape in the spotlight - and monkeyshines!

Q: Why should you always refuse to lend an ape money?

A: It's dangerous to let him put the bite on you!

Q: Why do waiters like gorillas better than flies?

A: Did you ever hear a customer complain: "Waiter, there's a gorilla in my soup!"

Q: Why do the gorillas like Jimmy Carter?

A: They don't really know - but they're NUTS about him!

Q: Why do apes like tall buildings?

A: They want to climb the heights of the business world!

Q: Why do apes climb to the tops of buildings?

A: The elevator men are on strike!

Q: Why did the gorilla visit Italy?

A: An advertisement headline enticed him - See Ape-les and die!

Q: Why did the gorilla fail English?

A: He had little ape-titude!

Q: Why did the gorilla enlist in the ragged continental army?

A: To avoid the draft!

Q: Why did the girl gorilla, engaged to the invisible man, call off the wedding?

A: Because in the last analysis she just couldn't see it!

Q: Why did the ape jump off the building?
A: He wanted to show the world the stuff he was made of!

Q: Why did the actor fire his gorilla agent?
A: The big ape wanted to take more than a 10% bite!

Q: Why did both Germany and the U.S want to hire apes during World War II?
A: Because they are excellent at waging gorilla-warfare!

Q: Why couldn't the gorilla pitcher make it in the major leagues?
A: His balk was worse than his bite!

Q: Why are gorillas underpaid?
A: They're willing to work for peanuts!

Q: Who is the gorillas favorite President of recent years?
A: Hairy Truman!

Q: Who is the gorilla's favorite playwright?
A: Eugene O'Neill - who wrote The Hairy Ape!

Q: Which wrestler do the gorillas admire most?

A: Gorilla Monsoon - he knows the ropes!

Q: Which two names figure prominently in every ape's diet?

A: Ben/Anna!

Q: Which technique does a gorilla borrow from another animal when it gets romantic?

A: The bear hug!

Q: Which operetta make the gorilla crack up?

A: Nutty Marietta!

Q: Which song title makes an ape heartsick?

A: Gorilla My Dreams!

Q: Which is the favorite gorilla proverb?
A: A fiend in need is a fiend indeed!

Q: Which drink makes a gorilla feel tipsy?
A: An ape-ricot sour!

Q: Which book makes prudish gorillas blush?

A: The Naked Ape!

Q: Which city holds the record for the most suicides committed by a gorilla jumping off a tall building?

A: Fall-adelphia!

Q: Which author do the gorillas love most?

A: John Steinbeck - who wrote The Apes of Wrath!

Q: Where did the gorilla play baseball?

A: In the bush leagues, of course!

Q: When did the gorillas start to picket the cookie factory?

A: The day they started to manufacture animal crackers!

Q: What's hairy and flies through the air?

A: Jonathan Livingstone Gorilla!

Q: What's black, hairy, and writes under water?

A: A ball-point gorilla!

Q: What's black, brown and white, black, brown and white, brown and white, etc.?

A: A gorilla riding down a snow bank!

Q: What political party entices most gorillas?
A: The Tree-publican Party!

Q: What is the ape monsters name?
A: Godzilla Gorilla!

Q: What happens if you cross an ape with an octopus?
A: You get a fur coat with lots of sleeves!

Q: What happens if you cross a parrot with a gorilla?
A: Nobody is sure, but if it opened its mouth to speak, you'd listen!

Q: What happened when the ape won the door prize?
A: He didn't take it - he already had a door!

Q: What gives a gorilla good taste?
A: Four years in an Ivy League school!

Q: What do they feed a gorilla when he goes to Paris?
A: Ape Suzettes!

Q: What did the great Ape shout to the pilots who tried to shoot him off the skyscraper?

A: Listen hotshots, don't monkey around with me!

Q: What did the great ape say as he plummeted from the skyscraper?

A: Listen baby, I think I'm falling for you!

Q: What did the gorilla do when he saw the sign, Clean Washroom?

A: He cleaned it!

Q: What did Mrs. Revere say when Paul got on a gorilla to warn the farmers that the British were coming?

A: Paul, stop monkeying around!

Q: What did George Washington have to do with gorillas?

A: As little as possible, dummy!

Q: If you put 30 female Apes and 30 male Apes in a bedroom, what do you have?

A: A very large bedroom.

Q: How do you stop a thundering herd of apes?

A: Hold up your arm and say, "Go back, you didn't say ‚May I?"

Q: How do you prepare a gorilla sundae?

A: Your start getting it ready Fridae and Saturdae!

Q: How do you make a gorilla float?

A: Two scoops of ice cream, some club soda and a very tasty gorilla!

Q: How do we know that Apes are like fish after a rainstorm?

A: They'll both bite at anything!

Q: How did the obscene telephone caller get attacked by the gorilla?

A: He made a mistake and dialed a preyer!

Q: How did the dog warn its master that a gorilla was approaching?

A: He barked g-r-r-r-illa!

Q: How did Gertie Gorilla win the beauty contest?

A: She was the beast of the show!

Q: How did Gertie Gorilla make the Playboy Calendar?

A: She was Miss Ape-ril!

Q: How did a Gorilla come to be with Washington at Valley Forge?

A: He had seen a sign saying, Uncle Simian Wants You!

Q: How come the giant ape climbed up the side of the skyscraper?

A: The elevator was broken!

Q: Do apes kiss?

A: Yes, but never on the first date!

Q: Do you know a favorite expression used by the gorillas?

A: Apesy-daisy!

Q: Why does Rilla get mad when he's in a race?

A: Because all his friends shout, GO-RILLA!

Pig Jokes

Q: Who do they get for Babe the Pig's dangerous movie scenes?

A: A stunt ham.

Q: What do you get when you cross a pig with a Billy goat?

A: A crashing bore.

Q: Why do pigs never recover from illness?

A: Because you have to kill them before you cure them!

Q: What kind of tie does a pig wear?

A: A pig's tie (pig sty)!

Q: What do you get if you cross pigs with a lot of grapes?

A: A swine gut!

Q: Why did the pig send his story to New York?

A: He wanted to be published on Pork Avenue.

Q: What are pigs warned to look out for in New York?

A: Pig pockets.

Q: Why was the pig happy when reviewers criticized his story?

A: Because they called it garbage.

Q: Why wouldn't the sow let her piglets play with toads?

A: She didn't want them to grow into wart hogs.

Q: Why wouldn't the piglet's mother let her read romantic novels?

A: She was afraid her daughter would run away with a wolf.

Q: Why wouldn't the bird let her chicks go near the pig pen?

A: She didn't want the pigs eating shredded tweet.

Q: Why won't the witch let the traveling pig actors into her gingerbread cottage?

A: She's afraid they'll bring down the house.

Q: Why won't pigs take up jogging?

A: They don't like to get that far from the table.

Q: Why should you never invite a pig to join your tug-of-war team?

A: Pigs want to be pulled through the mud hole.

Q: Why isn't there a Super Pig?

A: It's too hard for a pig to change clothes in a telephone booth.

Q: Why is your dad chasing those pigs through the garden?

A: We're raising mashed potatoes.

Q: Why is the cook worried about catching his runaway pig?

A: He knows a little ham goes a long way.

Q: Why was the pig unhappy in the Minors?

A: Because he wants to play in the Pig Leagues.

Q: Why is a pig in a water trough like a penny?

A: Because its head is on one side and its tail is on the other.

Q: Why doesn't Santa hitch his sleigh to a pig?

A: Pigs don't have red noses.

Q: Why do pigs love Halloween?

A: There's lots of hogsgobblin.

Q: Why do pigs like February 14th?

A: They get lots of Valenswines.

Q: Why didn't the pigs eat the rotten eggs in their feed trough?

A: They were saving the best for last.

Q: Why didn't the piglets listen to the teacher pig?

A: Because he was an old boar.

Q: Why didn't the Bionic Pig get a TV series of his own?

A: He made the mistake of going to a barbecue with Bionic Man and Bionic Woman.

Q: Why did the spotted pigs run away?

A: They thought the traveling salesman told the farmer to put his name on the dotted swine.

Q: Why did the pigs paint their hooves green?

A: It was Saint Pigtrick's Day.

Q: Why did the piglets get in trouble in their stained glass class?

A: They stained it with mud.

Q: Why did the piglets get in trouble in their biology class?

A: They ate all the specimens.

Q: Why did the piglets do badly in school?

A: They were all slow loiners.

Q: Why did the pig wear yellow coveralls?

A: He split a seam in his blue ones.

Q: Why did the pig run away from the pig sty?

A: He felt that the other pigs were taking him for grunted.

Q: Why did the pig join the Army?
A: He heard the food was a mess.

Q: Why did the pig go to the casino?
A: To play the slop machine!

Q: Why did the pig join a muscle-building class?
A: He thought pumping iron was a new juice dispenser.

Q: Why did the little piglet fall in love with the hog?
A: Because he was such a sloppy dresser.

Q: Why did the little pig try to join the Navy?
A: He loved to sing, Oinkers Aweigh.

Q: Why did the little pig hide the soap?
A: He heard the farmer yell, "Hogwash!"

Q: Why did the big pig want to go on stage?
A: There was a lot of ham in him.

Q: Why do pigs have flat snouts?
A: From running into trees.

Q: Why couldn't the pig pay his bill?
A: He was a little shoat.

Q: Why can't there be a Santa Pig?
A: Pigs don't fit in chimneys.

Q: Why are there so many piggy banks?
A: Pigs don't like to hide their money in the mattress.

Q: Why are pigs such great football fans?
A: They're always rooting and grunting.

Q: Who sends flowers on Valentine's Day?
A: Cupigs!

Q: Why are pigs such early risers?
A: Did you ever try to shut off a rooster?

Q: Who is the greatest painter of this century?
A: Pigcasso!

Q: Which of these jokes do the pigs like best?
A: The corniest ones.

Q: Where is the most open green space in New York City?

A: Central Pork

Q: Where does a woodsman keep his pigs?

A: In his hog cabin!

Q: Where do retired pigs go for warm weather?

A: The tropigs!

Q: Where do bad pigs go?

A: They get sent to the pen.

Q: Where did the piglets study their ABCs?

A: At a school for higher loining.

Q: When pigs have a party, who jumps out of the cake?

A: Nobody. The pigs all jump in.

Q: When pigs get toothaches, who do they see?

A: Painless Porker.

Q: When is a pig an ecologist?

A: When he recycles garbage into ham.

Q: What's that pig doing in the middle of the road with a red light on its head?

A: Didn't you tell me to put out a stop swine?

Q: What would happen if pigs went on strike?

A: They'd form pigget lines.

Q: What would happen if pigs could fly?

A: Bacon would go up!

Q: What would a pig name a chain of food stores?

A: Stop-n- Slop Markets.

Q: What world athletic sporting event is held every four years?

A: The Olympigs!

Q: What was the name of the hog who was knighted by King Arthur?

A: Sir Lunchalot.

Q: What soft drink do pigs like best?

A: Root beer.

Q: What should you say to a pig on roller skates?

A: Don't say anything. Just get out of the way.

Q: What position does the pig play in football?

A: Loinback.

Q: What kind of furniture do pigs like best?

A: Overstuffed.

Q: What kind of pig does a sow dislike?

A: Male chauvinist pigs.

Q: What kind of bread do pig ladles make in the Yukon?

A: Sow-r-dough bread.

Q: What is the pig's favorite musical instrument?

A: The piggalo (piccalo).

Q: What is a pig's favorite ballet?

A: Swine Lake!

Q: What is Chuck Norris' best karate move?

A: Pork Chop!

Q: What instrument do pigs play in a band?
A: Pigcussion!

Q: What goes knio, knio?
A: A backward pig.

Q: What does a pig use to write his term papers with?
A: Pen and oink!

Q: What do you say to a naked pig?
A: I never sausage a body.

Q: What do you give a sick pig?
A: Oinkment!

Q: What do you get when you cross a pig with an elephant?
A: A very large animal that knows a lot of jokes.

Q: What do you do for a pig with sore muscles?
A: Rub him with oinkment.

Q: What do you call the story of The Three Little Pigs?
A: A pig tail (tale)!

Q: What do you call pigs in a demolition derby?

A: Crashing boars.

Q: What do you call an oversized motorcycle for pigs?

A: A hog's hog.

Q: What do you call a pig with the flu?

A: A swine swine.

Q: What do you call a pig with no legs?

A: A groundhog!

Q: What do you call a pig with good table manners?

A: Sick.

Q: What do you call a pig with no clothes on?

A: Streaky bacon!

Q: What do you call a pig who overacts?

A: A ham ham.

Q: What do you call a pig thief?

A: A hamburglar!

Q: What do you call a pig that took a plane?
A: Swine flu!

Q: What do you call a pig in a steel foundry?
A: A pig pig.

Q: What do you call a lady pig planting seeds?
A: A sow sow.

Q: What do you call a crafty pig?
A: Cunning ham.

Q: What do pigs like with chow mein?
A: Sooey sauce.

Q: What do pigs do on nice afternoons?
A: They go on pignics.

Q: What do pigs drive?
A: Pig-up trucks!

Q: What do pigs take when they are sick?
A: Pigicillin!

Q: What do little pigs want to be when they grow up?

A: Garbage collectors.

Q: What do little piglets do on a Saturday night?

A: Have a pigjama party!

Q: What do hip pigs call their ladies?

A: Fine swine.

Q: What did the pig say when the wolf grabbed her tail?

A: That's the end of me!

Q: What did the pig say when it found a fly in its soup?

A: Yum yum.

Q: What did the pig say when his brother rolled on him?

A: Heavy!

Q: What did the pig do when a beetle landed in his feed trough?

A: He ate it quickly before the others could ask him to share.

Q: What did Mama Pig say when Junior Pig bought a basket of wormy apples?

A: Don't tell the farmer. He might charge us extra.

Q: What did the Mama Pig say to her bad little piglet?

A: Behave or Frankenswine will get you.

Q: What did the fat pig say when the farmer dumped corn mash into the trough?

A: I'm afraid that's all going to waist (waste).

Q: Two pigs robbed a bank. Why were they caught so quickly?

A: They squealed on each other.

Q: The hog was a failure as a TV talk show host. What happened?

A: He turned out to be a big boar.

Q: What is the pig's favorite Shakespeare play?

A: Hamlet.

Q: Is lunch the favorite subject of piglets?

A: No, it's theatre. They love to ham it up and hog all the attention.

Q: Is it true the pigs went over Niagara Falls in a barrel?

A: No, that story's just a lot of hogwash.

Q: If you drop this book in a pig pen, what should you do?

A: Take the words out of their mouths.

Q: I told you not to let those pigs in my office.

A: Now, look what's happened. They've eaten all the dates off my calendar!

Q: How does a pig write home?
A: With a pig pen.

Q: How does a Mama Pig put her piglets to sleep?

A: She reads them pig tales.

Q: How do you take a pig to the hospital?
A: By hambulance!

Q: How do you fit more pigs on your farm?

A: Build a sty-scraper!

Q: How did the little pig win at Monopoly?
A: He built hotels on Pork Place.

Q: How can you tell that the pig failed at being a good Easter bunny?

A: By the egg on its face.

Q: How can you recognize a Gnome Pig?

A: They're the ones with the little red hats.

Q: Have you heard about the pig who took up disco dancing?

A: He liked to swing his weight around.

Q: Do pigs like Backgammon?

A: No, they prefer their backs scratched.

Q: Did you hear the story about the razorback hog?

A: It's pretty dull.

Q: Did you hear of the pig that began hiding garbage in November?

A: She wanted to do her Christmas slopping early.

Q: Did you hear about the pigs who took up motorcycling?

A: They wanted to catch bugs with their teeth.

Q: Did you hear about the pig who tried to start a hot-air balloon business?

A: He couldn't get it off the ground.

Q: Did you hear about the pig that opened a pawn shop?

A: He called it Ham Hocks.

Rabbit Jokes

Q: What do you get when you cross a perm with a rabbit?

A: Curly hare.

Q: What do you get if you pour boiling water down rabbit holes?

A: Hot, cross bunnies!

Q: Why is a bunny the luckiest animal in the world?

A: It has four rabbit's feet.

Q: Why do rabbits go to the beauty parlor?

A: For hare care.

Q: Why did the rabbits go on strike?

A: They wanted better celery!

Q: Why did the rabbit have trouble hopping?

A: Because he always kept one foot in his pocket for good luck!

Q: Why did the rabbit run out of the fast-food restaurant?

A: He thought he heard someone order a quarter pounder on a toasted bunny.

Q: Why did the bald man paint rabbits on his head?

A: Because from a distance they looked like hares!

Q: Why couldn't the rabbit fly home for Easter?

A: He didn't have the hare fare.

Q: Why are rabbits never gold?

A: How would you tell them apart from goldfish?

Q: Why are rabbits like calculators?

A: They both multiply a lot.

Q: Which rabbits were famous bank robbers?

A: Bunny and Clyde.

Q: Which rabbit was in Western movies?

A: Hop along Cassidy.

Q: Which rabbit was a famous female aviator?
A: Amelia Harehart.

Q: Which rabbit is a famous comedian?
A: Bob Hop.

Q: Which rabbit stole from the rich to give to the poor?
A: Rabbit Hood.

Q: Where do rabbits settle their legal disputes?
A: In a pellet court!

Q: When does a rabbit go exactly as fast as a train?
A: When it's on the train.

Q: Where do rabbits go after their wedding?
A: On their bunnymoon.

Q: When do rabbits have buck teeth?
A: When their parents won't get them braces.

Q: What's the fastest way to send a rabbit?
A: Haremail.

Q: What's the best way to catch a unique rabbit?

A: Unique up on him

Q: What's a rabbit's favorite car?
A: Any make, just as long it's a hunchback!

Q: What's a rabbit's favorite TV show?
A: Hoppy Days.

Q: What's a rabbit's favorite song?
A: Hoppy Birthday to You.

Q: What's a rabbit's favorite musical?
A: Hare.

Q: What's a rabbit's favorite movie?
A: Rabbits of the Lost Ark.

Q: What's a rabbit's favorite book?
A: Hop on Pop.

Q: What's a rabbit's favorite dance?
A: The bunny hop.

Q: What weighs 35 tons, has four fuzzy ears, and is 80 million years old?
A: Two rabbits riding a brontosaurus.

Q: What should a rabbit use to keep his fur neat?
A: A harebrush.

Q: What must a policeman have before searching a rabbit's home?
A: A search warren!

Q: What kind of cars do rabbits drive?
A: Hop rods.

Q: What job do rabbits at hotels have?
A: Bellhop.

Q: What is the difference between a crazy bunny and a counterfeit banknote?
A: One is bad money and the other is a mad bunny!

Q: What does a bunny use when it goes fishing?
A: A harenet.

Q: What do you get when you cross a rabbit with strawberry soda?
A: A berry bubbly bunny.

Q: What do you get when you cross a rabbit with an elephant?

A: An elephant who never forgets to eat his carrots.

Q: What do you get when you cross a rabbit with a millionaire?

A: A bunny with money.

Q: What do you get when you cross a rabbit with a boy scout?

A: A boy scout who helps little old ladies hop across the street.

Q: What do you get when you cross a frog and a rabbit?

A: A rabbit that says, ribbit.

Q: What do you get when you cross a bunny with an orange?

A: A pip squeak.

Q: What do you get when you cross a bunny with a spider?

A: A harenet.

Q: What do you get when you cross a bunny with a leek?

A: A bunion.

Q: What do you get when you cross a bumble bee with a rabbit?
A: A honey bunny.

Q: What do you call the everyday routines of rabbits?
A: Rabbit habits.

Q: What do you call it when one rabbit challenges another rabbit to hop across a forty-yard canyon?
A: A hare dare.

Q: What do you call an unusual rabbit?
A: A rare hare.

Q: What do you call an ugly rabbit that sits on someone's forehead?
A: Unsightly facial hare!

Q: What do you call an operation on a rabbit?
A: A hare-cut.

Q: What do you call an easy-going rabbit?
A: Hoppy-go-lucky.

Q: What do you call an affectionate rabbit?
A: A tender, loving hare.

Q: What do you call a rabbit who works in a bakery?

A: A yeaster bunny!

Q: What do you call a rabbit who tells jokes?

A: A funny bunny!

Q: What do you call a rabbit that plays with foxes?

A: A dumb bunny!

Q: What do you call mobile homes for rabbits?

A: Wheelburrows!

Q: What do you call a man with a rabbit up his jumper?

A: Warren!

Q: What do you call a dumb bunny?

A: A hare brain.

Q: What do you call a rabbit with fleas?

A: Bugs Bunny.

Q: What do you call a rabbit with no clothes on?

A: A bare hare.

Q: What do you call a rabbit that is real cool?

A: A hip hopper.

Q: What do you call a chocolate Easter bunny that was out in the sun too long?

A: A runny bunny.

Q: What do rabbits put in their computers?

A: Hoppy disks!

Q: What did the rabbit bride get on her wedding day?

A: A forty-carrot wedding ring.

Q: What did the naughty rabbit leave for Easter?

A: Deviled eggs!

Q: What did the magician say when he made his rabbit disappear?

A: Hare today, gone tomorrow.

Q: What did the customer say to the pet shop assistant after buying a bunny?

A: Rabbit up nicely, it's a gift!

Q: What did the bunny want to do when he grew up?

A: Join the Hare Force.

Q: What did the bunny say when he only had thistles to eat?

A: Thistle have to do!

Q: What book did the rabbit take on vacation?

A: One with a hoppy ending.

Q: What are four hundred rabbits hopping backwards?

A: A receding hare line.

Q: May I buy half a rabbit?

A: No, we don't split hares!

Q: How is a rabbit like a plum?

A: They're both purple, except for the rabbit.

Q: How far can a rabbit run into the woods?

A: Halfway. After that she's running out of the woods.

Q: How do you make a rabbit stew?
A: Keep it waiting.

Q: How do you make a rabbit fast?
A: Don't feed it.

Q: How do you know when you're eating rabbit stew?
A: When it has hares in it.

Q: How do you know when there's a rabbit in your bed?
A: You can smell the carrots on his breath.

Q: How do rabbits get to work?
A: By rabbit transit!

Q: How did the rabbit become a wrestling champion?
A: It had a lot of hare pins!

Q: How did the close race between the rabbit and the tortoise end?
A: It was won by a hare!

Q: How can you tell which rabbits are the oldest in a group?
A: Look for gray hares.

Skunk Jokes

Q: What did one skunk say to another?
A: And so do you!

Q: What happened to the skunk who failed his swimming lesson?
A: He stank to the bottom of the pool!

Q: What do you call a flying skunk?
A: A smellicopter!

Q: What do you get if you cross a skunk and an owl?
A: A bird that stinks, but doesn't give a hoot!

Q: What is the feeling that you've smelled a certain skunk before?
A: Deja-phew!

Q: What did the judge say when the skunk was on trial?
A: Odor in court!

Q: What do you get if you cross a skunk and a balloon?

A: A creature that stinks to high heaven!

Q: Did you hear about the argumentative skunk?

A: He always liked to make a stink!

Q: Did you hear about the skunk who sat on a fan?

A: He got cut off without a scent!

Q: When should you feel sorry for a skunk?

A: When its spray pump is out of order!

Q: What do you get if you cross a skunk and a cartoon penguin?

A: Pingu-Pong!

Q: How are skunks able to avoid danger?

A: By using their instinks and common scents!

Q: What do you get if you cross a skunk and a wasp?

A: Something that stinks and stings!

Q: Why was the skunk angry?
A: He was incensed!

Q: Why did the skunk buy four boxes of tissues?
A: Because he had a stinking cold!

Q: What's a skunk's philosophy on life?
A: Eat, stink, and be merry!

Q: What did the baby skunk want to be when he grew up?
A: A big stinker!

Q: What do you get if you cross a skunk and a boomerang?
A: A smell that keeps coming back!

Q: What's a skunk's favorite game in school?
A: Show and smell!

Q: How can you tell a rabbit from a skunk?
A: A skunk uses a cheaper deodorant!

Q: How can you tell when a skunk is angry?
A: It raises a stink!

Q: What do you get if you cross a skunk and a dinosaur?
A: A stinkasaurus!

Q: How many skunks do you need to make a house really smelly?
A: Just a phew!

Q: Did you hear the joke about the skunk?
A: Never mind, it stinks!

Other Animal Jokes

Q: What kind of tiles can walk?
A: Reptiles!

Q: What do headmasters and bullfrogs have in common?
A: Both have big heads that consist mostly of mouth!

Q: What's the definition of a nervous breakdown?
A: A chameleon on a tartan rug!

Q: What powerful reptile is found on a movie?
A: The Lizard of Oz!

Q: Why did the tadpole feel lonely?
A: Because he was new to the area!

Q: What is a chameleon's motto?
A: A change is as good as a rest!

Q: What was the name of the film about a killer lion that swam underwater?
A: Claws.

Q: What is the fiercest flower in the garden?
A: The tiger lily!

Q: What happened when the lion ate the comedian?
A: He felt funny!

Q: What do tigers wear in bed?
A: Striped pajamas!

Q: What did the lions say to his cubs when he taught them to hunt?
A: Don't go over the road till you see the zebra crossing.

Q: What flies around your light at night and can bite off your head?
A: A tiger moth!

Q: When is a lion not a lion?
A: When he turns into his cage!

Q: How are tigers like sergeants in the army?
A: They both wear stripes!

Q: What do you get if you cross a tiger with a kangaroo?

A: A striped jumper!

Q: What do you get if you cross a tiger with a sheep?

A: A striped sweater!

Q: What happened to the cheetah that took a bath three times a day?

A: After a week he was spotless!

Q: What's the difference between a tiger and a lion?

A: A tiger has the mane part missing!

Q: Why was the lion-tamer fined?

A: He parked on a yellow lion!

Q: What happened to the man who tried to cross a lion with a goat?

A: He had to get a new goat!

Q: How does a leopard change its spots?

A: When it gets tired of one spot it just moves to another!

Q: What do you call a show full of lions?

A: The mane event!

Q: What do you call a lion wearing a flower in its mane?
A: A dandy lion!

Q: What do you get if you cross a skunk with a bear?
A: Winnie the Pooh!

Q: What do you get if you cross a grizzly bear and a harp?
A: A bear faced liar (lyre)!

Q: What do polar bears have for lunch?
A: Ice burgers!

Q: How do you start a teddy bear race?
A: Ready, teddy, go!

Q: What do you call a big white bear with a hole in his middle?
A: A polo bear!

Q: What is a bear's favorite drink?
A: Coca-Koala!

Q: Why is polar bear cheap to have as a pet?
A: It lives on ice!

Q: How do you hire a teddy bear?
A: Put him on stilts!

Q: What do you get if you cross a teddy bear with a pig?
A: A teddy boar!

Q: Why do bears have fur coats?
A: Because they'd look stupid in leather jackets!

ABOUT THE AUTHOR

The Joke King, Johnny B. Laughing is a best-selling joke book author. He is a jokester at heart and enjoys a good laugh, pulling pranks on his friends, and telling funny and hilarious jokes!

For more funny joke books just search for:

Visit the website:

www.funny-jokes-online.weebly.com

Johnny B. Laughing *"The Joke King"*

Made in the USA
Coppell, TX
20 December 2021

69598684R00098